Interior D
50 Tips for Beginners to Home Decorating on a Budget (Complete Guide to Interior Designing)

Richard Foreman

PUBLISHED BY:

Richard Foreman

Copyright © 2015

Visit our website to get more books information:

justhappyforever.com

All rights reserved.

No part of this publication may be copied, reproduced in any format, by any means, electronic or otherwise, without prior consent from the copyright owner and publisher of this book.

Disclaimer

The information contained in this ebook is for general information purposes only. The information is provided by the authors and while we endeavor to keep the information up to date and correct, we make no representations or warranties of any kind, express or implied, about the completeness, accuracy, reliability, suitability or availability with respect to the ebook or the information, products, services, or related graphics contained in the ebook for any purpose. Any reliance you place on such information is therefore strictly at your own risk.

WAIT! Before you continue…

Just to say thank you for purchasing this book, I want to give you a 100% FREE GIFT (valued at $5.99): *10 Hot Tips for Eating Right & Losing Weight Fast.*

You will get the tips for eating right and losing weight fast to make you health.

Click here to access your Free gift

Table of Contents

Introduction

Chapter 1: Basic: Interior Design Principles You Need To Know

Chapter 2: Homes that Radiate Luxury and Elegance

Chapter 3: Five Fundamental Basics of Interior Designing

Chapter 4: Color Psychology to Spruce up Emotions

Chapter 5: The Essential Tool for All Home Stylists Choosing Room Colors for Your Home

Chapter 6: Keeping Home Makeovers within Budget

Chapter 7: Preparing Your Space for an Uplift

Chapter 8: Knowing More about Different Interior Design Styles

Chapter 9: Gathering your Samples and Making a Design Clipboard

Chapter 10: 50 Interior Design Tips for Beginners

- Tip 1 – Color schemes
- Tip 2 – Pieces that fit your space
- Tip 3 – Buy chairs and table separately
- Tip 4 – Careful choice of lighting
- Tip 5 – Use of illumination
- Tip 6 – Use muted colors
- Tip 7 – Using pieces with historic interest
- Tip 8 – Golds, silvers and metallic colors
- Tip 9 – The rule of threes
- Tip 10 – The addition of rugs
- Tip 11 – Use mirrors wisely
- Tip 12 – Family photos
- Tip 13 – Buy quality
- Tip 14 – Invest in artwork
- Tip 15 – Add period drama

Tip 16 – Plump up the cushions

Tip 17 – De-clutter

Tip 18 – Keep window treatments simple

Tip 19 – Color tips

Tip 20 – Make your home a treasure trove

Tip 21 – Move things around

Tip 22 – Update furniture

Tip 23 – Use shapes that enhance your space

Tip 24 – Simple and functional

Tip 25 – Change the handles

Tip 26 – Colors for a warmer room

Tip 27 – Buy sufficient materials

Tip 28 – Use your design clipboard

Tip 29 – Look for natural inspiration

Tip 30 – If in doubt, leave it out

Tip 31 – Add textures

Tip 32 – Ceiling colors

Tip 33 – Using neutrals

Tip 34 – Paint bold pieces

Tip 35 – Using color to calm

Tip 36 – Layering the look

Tip 37 – Add vibrance

Tip 38 – Try prints

Tip 39 – Opposing textures

- Tip 40 – Use of grey
- Tip 41 – Design and color for class
- Tip 42 – Use artwork for inspiration
- Tip 43 – Calm the ceilings
- Tip 44 – Use of florals
- Tip 45 – Mix new with old
- Tip 46 – Creating interest
- Tip 47 – Dark colors
- Tip 48 – Natural light
- Tip 49 – Accent colors
- Tip 50 – avoid op-art

Chapter 11: Simple Preparation Tips to Help You to Create Perfect Walls and Ceilings

- Tools required for preparation:
- Examination of the surfaces
- Where baseboard and wall meet
- To get rid of stains on ceilings

Chapter 12: Making Great Savings on Design Elements

Chapter 13: What Is Feng Shui Decorating?

Chapter 14: Tips For Decorating Your Home On A Budget

Chapter 15: Feng Shui Decorating Ideas For Your Living Room

Chapter 16: Feng Shui Decorating Ideas For Your Kitchen

Chapter 17: Feng Shui Decorating Ideas For Your Bedroom Makeover

Chapter 18: Methods To Organizing Your Home

Chapter 19: Declutter Your Life & Home in 5 Simple Steps

Chapter 20: DIY Home Decorating Ideas

Chapter 21: Modern Painting Techniques

Conclusion

Introduction

With a little imagination, you really can design the interior of your home to suit your own style. It doesn't always take spending a fortune. This book is geared toward those that want their homes to look designer style on a budget. Believe it or not, you really can improve what you home looks like by understanding basic design principles.

And this is what this book aims to do. Stop complaining and start moving with easy to follow tips on how you can get started on decorating your dream home to your own specification. It's easier than you might imagine and cheaper too!

This book contains proven steps and strategies on how to decorate your home without breaking the bank. From interior design principles, to color psychology, and even tips on how and where to start, you're sure to learn everything you need to know about basic interior design in this book.

The basic idea here is that the environment we're in affects us greatly and as such, we need to pay more attention to it. Feng Shui would not only help us boost the positive energy in our homes, but also bring about harmony. All of which would benefit those living within the space.

A handful tips that will surely help you in addressing design issues usually encountered by designers during the design process are also to be found and discovered in this book.

Chapter 1: Basic: Interior Design Principles You Need To Know

Interior design is basically the method used for improving the overall experience of an interior space. Just by following some simple guidelines and honing in on your creativity, you can easily turn any space into your own. Although it would probably take you years to become an interior design expert, knowing the following basic principles can help you keep on the right track. These are simplified so that you gain a great understanding of interior decorating principles as used by designers. These can be easily incorporated into the way that you view your home renovation or decorating project.

Unity and Harmony

When designing the interiors of your home, you need to look at the whole house in its entirety. The design of each room should work in unison with the overall feel of the home. Think of your home as a series of spaces being linked together by hallways and stairways. It's not advisable to decorate one room in one theme and decorate the others in a completely different theme. To get a cohesive look for your entire home, it's important that you have a common style or theme run through the different rooms. Interior designer elements should work together and complement the overall feel of your home.

The transition between one room and the next comes into the designer package. Supposing for example, you used clashing colors in adjoining rooms. It would look badly put together whenever the doors are open between the two rooms. This is why an overall style is chosen before you start

Balance

Balance can be best described as the equal distribution of visual interest in a room. There are 3 ways you can achieve balance in your interior design: asymmetrical, symmetrical and radial.

Symmetrical balance is more traditional and is considered to be the safest. You can achieve this effect by putting two of the same things on each side of the room. So if you have a nightstand on one side of a bed, symmetrical balance requires that you put the same on the other side. Symmetry is the easiest way to achieve balance in any room design. This could be achieved with artwork, ornament or even decoration. Two alcoves at either side of a fireplace can be balanced off nicely by decorating them in the same kind of colors, so that the focal point is the actual fireplace, but the symmetry of the room is maintained.

Asymmetrical balance on the other hand is more modern and lively. To achieve this effect, dissimilar objects are used to add visual weight to a room. So instead of adding another nightstand on the other side of the bed, you can maybe add a large mirror to achieve that sense of balance. The feel of this style is very casual, but it can get a bit too casual, especially if the design elements are not thought out properly. This form of decoration is very popular with young people who may have open plan spaces. By using this, the rules change and a wall of colorful wallpaper can be introduced to highlight an actual area of the room, rather than trying to balance the look by using the same décor.

Radial balance is achieved when elements are arranged around a central point. This is the least commonly used style since it requires a large space in order to be executed well. However, you can do this in a small room if you are clever about the content that you put into the room. For example, smaller furniture in a smaller room gives the impression that the room is larger.

Emphasis

Every well designed room needs to have at least one focal point. A focal point is that area in a room that doesn't just draw attention to it, but it should also create a lasting impression. In some homes, the focal point can be a fireplace, while in others, its windows. To create a natural focal point in your home, look for that area that is highly visible. Then place an interesting piece of furniture, or artwork that you want to highlight in that area. Make sure to maintain room balance so that your focal point doesn't end up hogging all the attention.

There is another way that you can establish which areas of rooms are currently the focal points. You may be disappointed to learn that the focal points that you are using actually highlight things you would prefer to hide. To establish what the current focal point is, close the door to a room. Then open the door and enter the room. What is the first thing that your eye is drawn to? This is the current focal point but if you change that focal point, you can make a small room look larger, a dark room look lighter and a large room look more intimate and cozy.

Rhythm

Rhythm in interior design refers to the design elements that lend visual interest through patterns or contrasts. It doesn't just add visual interest to a room, but it also makes it more interesting to look at. Think of it like telling a story. Your room should have surprising details to make it more appealing. If you want to show movement or rhythm in a room, you have 4 methods that you can use: repetition, transition, progression, and contrast. Repetition is when you use the same pattern, color, or texture in a space more than once. Using the same shade of yellow in your curtains to match a yellow rug in the same room is the perfect example of repetition. This is the easiest way to pull together the look of a room.

This is achieved by making yourself a design board. It may sound fancy, but it isn't. It's a clip board to which you add little pieces of potential fabric for curtains, photos of furniture which is of a set color that you can't change and paint colors to be used to go with all of those items. Having them together on a board allows you to cut out magazine snippets and ideas to give you the overall look within the repetition style, if this is what you want to achieve.

Transition on the other hand shows a much smoother flow. This method takes advantage of the viewer's natural eye movement and arranges design elements in a way that it allows the eyes to glide from one area to the next. An arched doorway or a winding path leads the eye to the next point of interest. This is why we mentioned earlier that it's so vital for adjoining rooms to be decorated in colors which go well together. When you open the door to the next room, the room can be painted in a complimentary shade of the same color. This is cheap to achieve if you buy white paint and then use colored pigments to mix your own paints with. The colors that you achieve will be unique and you can keep a jam jar of each color as and when you finish a room, so that you have touch up paint if any is needed. Wear and tear can be kept to a minimum using this method.

Progression is when you use a design element in different sizes and color shades to decorate your space. Take for example a cluster of candles of different sizes to decorate your fireplace mantel, or using a monochromatic color scheme in different shades to make your room look more vibrant. The eye is drawn toward these progressions and from a bedroom through to a romantic bathroom, the ideas that you incorporate really can make a huge difference to how people perceive that space.

Contrast is bold and very straightforward. It's when you put together design elements that obviously oppose one another. The best example of this is using black and white throw pillows together on the couch, or using circle and square pillows together to liven up a space. Op art or opposite art colors were popular in the 1960s but have recently come back into style. Contrasting pillows, light fittings or ornaments use very bold colorings that contrast with the main wall colors.

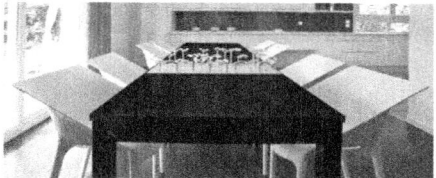

In the above image, look how startlingly effective the design is, using black and white as the main colors for the scheme. You may not be able to afford designer chairs such as this, but you may still be able to create a room that uses contrast in every bit as an effective way. Image from Flicker by Home and Stlye

Proportion and Scale

Proportion and scale go hand in hand because they both relate to the size of your design elements. You want your room to look just right - not too big or too small. Decorating a big room allows you to use larger pieces. If you're working with a small room, you should use design elements that aren't overpowering to the space. Many people make the mistake of trying to sell homes that are filled with clutter. What this does is give the buyers the impression that they have outgrown the space. That's what happens when you have a lot of items within a room. Thin down where possible, because less, in the field of home design, is often more.

By learning these design principles and how they go together, you'll be able to put together a room that you can be proud of. The next step is to add a bit of color into the mix. In the next chapter, you'll learn the basic psychology of color, and you can choose which colors to incorporate into your space as well as learning how to make up a design clipboard so that you can gather fabric colors, images and paint colors together to see what the end result is likely to be.

Chapter 2: Homes that Radiate Luxury and Elegance

There are numerous ways to incorporate your personality when designing an elegant home; not every luxury home is entitled to one type of design. Here are a few popular designs to achieve an elegant and luxurious home:

Parisian

A French interior is always classy and elegant. With a luxurious touch, which is what France is known for, your home will always feel comfortable and sophisticated. A Parisian inspired abode is all about incorporating the old with the new in a fresh, refined way.

Instead of making every object in an area match its theme, a French interior allows distinctive and unique pieces to complement one another without overdoing it. In turn, it creates an artistic harmony that anyone would enjoy. Image from Flicker by Stylish Art

Tuscan

Tuscan is a city located in the countryside of Italy. It also has its own unique style derived from the simple locale. Nonetheless, styles that encompass the minimal characteristics of Tuscan usually bring an air of luxury and elegance with it.

A Tuscan inspired interior encompasses a rustic environment featuring earthy tones with refined wrought-iron accents, textured walls, and terracotta tiles. Image from Flicker by Italian Style Homes

Asian

Reminiscent of Japanese and Chinese culture, an Asian inspired interior contains simple oriental accessories that can help you slip into a state of peace and tranquility. These may include calligraphy, woven straw mats, bamboo finishes, floral designs, and low furniture.

With exotic décor such as these, an Asian styled home is always an elegant choice for anyone who wants a taste of a gracious culture. Image from Flicker by Frederick Homes Deco

Chapter 3: Five Fundamental Basics of Interior Designing

It is essential for you to know the five fundamental basics that make up a well-designed interior. Combined and used correctly, these basics provide a complete room of harmony and peace.

Unity

Each and every room in a house should have its own theme and mood. Whatever it is, it should unify the whole room, and not emanate separate ideas—stick to one theme or use complementary themes. If you wish for a modern and monochromatic bedroom, adding in features such as dark, wooden chairs will throw off the whole premise you desired.

Rhythm

In terms of interior design, rhythm is using a certain repeating or progressive pattern. An example of patterned rhythm in a living room is the use of the same colors in the pillows, picture frames, and rug. This way, you will evenly distribute the pattern throughout the space. Even using opposite or contrasting colors can establish a perfect pattern.

On the other hand, a progressive rhythm includesusing various sizes of candles on your bathtub—a small one, medium-sized one, and large one. In this way, the sizes of the candles are progressively growing, which adds contrast to the room.

Sense of balance

An area containing numerous décor that are visually heavy—such as large vases or statues—may put you in a "heavy" mood also. Any room should have a sense of balance. You can achieve this by placing different adornments of various size, weight, texture, brightness and design throughout the room. The key is to mix heavy objects with light ones to keep the room at equilibrium.

Proportion

Frankly, the larger rooms of the house should contain furniture that are also big, while smaller-sized rooms should possess smaller-sized furniture. If you place a king-sized bed in a small bedroom, the area will feel smaller.

Highlight

There should be at least one focal point in every room. It could be a piece of artwork or a piece of furniture; anything that can draw the eyes of people will do nicely. Particular groupings of furniture, alluring embellishments, and unusual or large objects can also work great as focal points for rooms

Chapter 4: Color Psychology to Spruce up Emotions

One of the fastest ways to change up the feel of your home is by incorporating color. Trends come and go, but color can give you that emotional attachment to your home. Use your design clipboard to gather samples of colors and fabrics as this will help you to be able to put effective colorings together.

Picking the right color may seem daunting, but if you pull this off well, you'll end up with a home that you can be proud of. The trick is to choose colors that will help you achieve that effect that you're going for. There are different ways to pick out color but the best way is to choose colors that don't just look good together, but also give you the right feel for your room.

The first thing that you need to understand about picking color is that you need to think of the psychological aspect of colors. You need to pick out colors that will not only appeal to you but also be appropriate for the room. Color is one of the best ways to achieve harmony in your overall home design so make sure to choose wisely.

As a rule of thumb, lighter shades of color can make a room look bigger, while darker shades give it that sophisticated feel. So aside from picking out a color you like, make sure to choose colors that would match the room's purpose and the desired overall look. Here's a list of colors and the effect they can have on your home.

Red

Red is a great choice if you want energy in a space. The warmness of red can draw people together and stimulate conversation. Although it may create a strong impression at first, you can offset this by incorporating neutrals in your color palette. Physically, red is known to raise blood pressure and heart rate so think twice before choosing this color for your bedroom. Red, however, would work perfectly for a living room or dining room space if you do a lot of entertaining.

If you examine the next photograph, you will note that the use of red was quite subtle and it added to the richness of the wood color of the furniture. This gives the room a traditional but well established classical look and that's what many new homes lack. Red can do that if you choose the shade of red carefully.

In this room setting, the red chosen is subdued. What that does is give the home a richness without being overstated. It warms the room and makes it very welcoming and the home owner has used the coloring of the wall to reflect into the picture frames on the wall of the opposing color. That's clever incorporation of color. If you can't afford the frames you want, you can always paint up old ones and use them. A simple coat of undercoat and topcoat and you will get great results.

Pink

Although pink is traditionally a color for girls — specifically young ones— it is still of great value. In fact, pink is the only color that doesn't leave a negative impact on the mind. Most guys aren't big fans of this bright color, however pink can bring forth happiness and romantic feelings. It can also reduce aggression. Baby pink or hot pink, you can use this in any room you wish.

Yellow

Yellow is fun, vibrant and happy - perfect for spaces that need brightness like the kitchen or bathroom. Yellow can be energizing and uplifting so if you have any odd spaces in your home that need a bit of life, then yellow is definitely the color. But be warned. Yellow may not have a calming effect on some people. Studies show that people are more likely to get into an argument and babies tend to cry more in a yellow room. So if you're going to incorporate yellow into your color scheme, make sure that it isn't overpowering or avoid the nursery altogether.

Yellow in a kitchen can look rather nice, though pale yellows are preferred. These open up a space and make it look clean and crisp which is why pale yellow is often used for a wall coloring in a bathroom or kitchen.

Blue

Blue gives off a relaxing and serene feel, making it perfect for your bedrooms or any room that you want to have a peaceful feel. The downside, however, is that a blue room can make it seem uninviting and chilly, especially if you're going to use a dark blue shade. The results can be sad and depressing if you don't offset it with some warmer colors. If you want blue to have a calming effect on your room, choose brighter or softer tones like periwinkle or cerulean as your main room color. Blues work best in rooms that receive lots of natural light.

For smart contrast between colors, white works well with blue and gives the whole area a very clean feel. Look at the image below and you will see how blue can be introduced without actually being the main shade in the room, although it still retains its dominance over the style of the room.

Green

Green is the color that is considered to be the most restful for the eyes, making it perfect for your family room or living room. If you're looking for a color that combines calming blue and cheery yellow, then this is perfect for you. Green gives that perfect balance of cool and happy so you can use it as a main color for decorating just about any room. This color helps relieve stress and gives your room a fresh feeling so it would definitely work well in a home office.

If you go back to the times of William Morris and the Arts & Crafts movement, green was commonly used because of its links with nature. Some of the most stunning rooms use the arts and crafts paper to this day and still look wonderful. If you can't afford to do a whole room, why not have a panel? You can make one by buying a plain frame and simply wallpapering on a piece of card large enough to be placed within that frame.

Making panels to fit the walls of your home also gives you instant artwork at a fraction of the price, so you can make your home look stylish even on a stretched budget.

Purple

Purple is dramatic, rich and sophisticated, making it perfect for rooms that you want a lot of creativity in. The dark shades make great accent colors, while the lighter shades can bring a restful feel to the bedroom. Since purple isn't actually a go to color for many designers, you can use it to add impact to an otherwise drab room.

In the style shown below, purple is used to give the room a very grown up look and although used in small quantities, actually adds an awful lot to the ambiance of the bathroom, with the colors softened by painted floorboards and white backdrop to match with the stylized bathtub. None of the decorative elements used need to be that expensive but they do create a very expensive look. Even if your perfume bottles or shampoo bottles are only used as decoration, having bottles with purple liquid in them helps to keep the whole look in harmony.

Orange

Orange is all about excitement and energy so you can use this color for the kitchen or the living room. It will also look great in the kids' play area. Although it's not a very good idea for the bedroom, it can do wonders in your exercise space. The cheery energetic color might just be the thing you need to get through the most tiring exercise routine. Imagine the richness of color in a Moroccan home and you will also be able to see that mixed with dark red, it can actually make the room look warm even on a winter's day, but be sure that the furnishings that you use are not overly colorful as this will mean that you have too much color in the room and this can confuse the style.

Brown

Along with the color green, brown is another shade of nature that can reduce stress. People also believe that this color can hold back emotions by giving a person a serene and comforting environment. In addition, brown is a symbol of strength. Use brown in your office or workroom, but lay off the color when painting your bedroom.

Black and White

Monochromatic colors such as black and white are always a classic touch to any home. White is simple and candid — virtually any household can use this color. It radiates a pure room and supplies the illusion of having a large space. Analogous to the first snow of the winter, wedding dresses, and clouds dotted over the sky, white is such a crisp and pristine color that will never get old. However, white can also give off the impression of an empty room. For this reason, skip the color white forliving rooms and children's rooms, and instead use it for the bathroom or kitchen.

Meanwhile, black radiates a sense of power and supremacy. Although it really is a bold and daring color, it can also give an impression of a negative environment. For this reason, use black in moderation, such as accents to an area. Nevertheless, if you truly desire to place all-black furniture as the main piece in an area or paint an entire wall black, keep in mind that using black after that should be at an all-time minimum. Instead, pair it with bright hues, such as yellow or a lime green.

Once you have extracted loads of inspiration and knowledge of color psychology, it's time to put them into play. Read further to learn how to create your own mood board.

Neutrals

To get the desired effect from your chosen colors, you also need to incorporate tried and tested neutrals into your palette. The great thing about choosing neutral colors is how flexible they can be. It allows you to use just about any color you want without coming off too overpowering. You can add black, gray, brown, or white accents to tone down a strong red room, or liven up a dark blue room. Adding neutral colors into the mix can give your room much needed depth.

Now that you've got colors sorted out, it's time to start planning that room makeover. But before you go on a buying spree, learn how you can keep your interior design project within budget. The next chapter will teach you the budgeting tricks that interior designers are not telling you about.

Chapter 5: The Essential Tool for All Home Stylists Choosing Room Colors for Your Home

Use the basic principles you learned about colors and qualities of a room to build a mood board. A mood board aids you in constructing the basic idea of your room. This tool is extremely essential for any interior designer, and plus, it's a fun part in the designing process.

Before you start making your mood board, you have to gain inspiration. Flip through pages of a home magazine and find pictures of designs you like. It is important that you establish a preferred design style that you wish your living space would embody. In this way, building a mood board won't be that much of a hassle.

The great thing about using a mood board is that it can consist of anything you like— fabrics, color scheme, art, pictures of furniture, etc. Think of it like a room on a board; it serves as a guide to visualize the final product of a living space, or a means to transfer your ideas onto a hard copy that you can edit later.

For an easy-to-edit mood board, why not go digital? You can use Pinterest to share your ideas with other people, you can even get helpful bits of advice from the online community. You can also browse other people's "boards" for additional inspiration for your projects.

It's quite difficult to tweak out your room when it is all finished—especially when you have already spent loads of cash on it. This is why a mood board is so handy. By possessing a visual representation of what your room will turn out to be, you can fix any problems easily.

The following are subjects that encompass a mood board:

Color Scheme

Creating a color scheme is enjoyable. There are plenty of color wheels online, or you can buy one at your local arts and crafts store. When laying colors on top of one another, it is crucial that the color schemes you pick are representations of complementary colors.

For elegant homes, the popular color schemes used are:

In any situation, using three colors to build your color scheme is genius. Building any room with three colors will promote harmony and a sense of stability. Just remember to distribute the colors evenly throughout the room to accomplish balance. For example, if you have pillows embroidered with blue detail, it would be a wise decision to have the same shade of blue in decorations on the wall or dresser.

Furniture

Flip through pages of a home design magazine or websites, whether new or old. In all probability, you will come across a particular piece of furniture that you must have. Once you see something you like, cut it or print it out and stick it on your mood board. Make sure that the furniture encompasses the interior design style you wish to accomplish.

When picking furnishings, you need to take into consideration the size of the space you are working with. This complies under one of the fundamental basics of interior designing, which is proportion.

Wallpaper or paint

Whether you want to use wallpaper or paint to spruce up your living space, you need to visualize it before proceeding. Some interior designers like to place a small square of paper, or sample, consisting of the desired paint or wallpaper they want to use. However, you can cover the whole mood board of the fabric or paint if you wish to really embody the whole feel of the room.

Flooring

Carpet is lush and comforting, while tiled or hardwood flooring can give an industrial feel. Decide whether you want your living space to have carpet or tiled floors.

Lighting

There is more to the illumination of a room than a mere light bulb. With hundreds of various and decorative lamps, chandeliers, and ceiling fans, the right design of lighting is very crucial to the interior of an area. Lighting is important since it highlights the detailsand contrast of a room. Good lighting should brighten up all corners of an area. To add lighting into your mood board, clip out a picture of main lighting—the lights that is installed into the ceiling—and indirect lighting—which is secondary lights like lamps—that you may like for your house.

Texture

Texture is an important principle that all interior designers touch up on. Textures can have smooth, rough, hard, matte, or shiny surfaces and they can add a lot of details and features. These can be found in wallpaper, decorations, and flooring, to name a few. For example, let's envision a room with white polished marble tiles. The furniture may include a smooth and shiny black dresser with polished adornments placed on top. If we reflect light inside the room, these furnishings will have a constant consistency of a glistening interior. But instead of going for one type of texture–which in this case, it's smooth and shiny–add in other textured surfaces as well, such as a rocky exterior or a matte dresser instead.

In conclusion, the samples you have pasted onto your mood board should have different textures. Look at a picture of a styled interior in magazines or on the Internet and examine the various textures it has. Your living areas should mirror that image as well.

Chapter 6: Keeping Home Makeovers within Budget

Whether you're remodeling an old space, or decorating a new one, there are ways to get amazing design effects without breaking the bank. Here are some tried and tested tips on how you can update your space without spending too much. These are general ideas for many of the rooms of your house, but putting it all together will be a fun exercise and we will give you more details on this in a later chapter.

Go online

You can access great deals and great ideas just by going online. From auction sites to furniture outlets, the Internet can give you the low-down on where to get the cheapest materials in your area. If you're lacking on creativity, you can get a bit of inspiration by checking out sites like Pinterest. Whenever you find yourself in doubt, just go online. One great site which gives you designs from all over the world is Houzz and on this website, you can collect images just like you would clip out pictures from magazines. These pictures are filled to brimming with ideas that you can incorporate without spending a lot of money. You may even be able to use existing furniture by sprucing it up a little.

Check out garage sales

As they say, one person's garbage can be another's treasure. Don't hesitate to check out garage sales in your neighborhood to see what kind of furniture or home fixtures you can get for your design project. If there aren't any garage sales happening, then the next best thing would be your local antique shop. Although some pieces may cost a bit more, antique shops have unique and interesting pieces that you won't be able to find anywhere else. Once you find something you like, don't forget to bargain for it and never pay the price marked. Nothing compares to the feeling of saving a few dollars here and there.

Visit wholesalers and outlet stores

If you want to get construction supplies like tiles, wallpaper or paint on the cheap, make sure to check out your local home outlet store for great deals. Ask to see discontinued items since these are often marked down dramatically. You can also check with wholesalers to see what materials you can get on a discount, especially if you're buying materials in bulk. Don't be afraid to ask about their return policy just in case you end up changing your mind about an item.

Something you can save money on is the items that a shop uses to demonstrate a style. If they have demo items, they often sell these when they change the décor in the shop and you can make some real savings. Look out for paints at all times, but always buy the best quality that you can afford as it will cover better and you will need less of it than you would if you bought cheap paint.

Check out cheaper alternatives

You don't have to splurge on materials to get the effect that you want so before you set your heart on that expensive printed wallpaper, do your research and check for cheaper alternatives. Don't blow off your whole budget just because you liked a specific fabric, or you can't do without those granite countertops. With countless choices out there, try not to settle for the first thing you see. Sometimes you can create a look without having to pay for the authenticity. If you can't afford designer wallpaper, why not limit the wallpaper to specific areas such as alcoves. You will still be able to incorporate it, but you will use less of it.

Refresh fixtures

Instead of buying new fixtures, check if you can refresh them instead. Scratches on tubs and sinks can be remedied by a touch of paint or some polishing. You can also check online for service providers who can resurface kitchen and bathroom fixtures if you don't have time to do it on your own. There are cabinet paints which are great for your kitchen units and if your husband takes all the doors and drawer fronts out to the garage at the weekend, you could end up with a new looking kitchen next week. You can always buy new handles which are relatively inexpensive to give the newly painted items a fresh look. At the same time, this may encourage you to clean out all those cabinets.

Get into refurbishing

Why buy new furniture when you still have decent pieces you can incorporate in your design? Replace certain parts, smoothen out dings, and repaint dated furniture with new and exciting colors. With a bit of creativity, you can easily bring old furniture back to life. There are some great ideas for painting furniture on sites like Pinterest but be very careful that the furniture you are choosing to paint does not have an anti que value, since some of this could be lost if you choose to paint it. Re-upholstery doesn't have to cost the earth. If you buy throws, these can be used to re-upholster a snug armchair and give it an up to date look.

Look at this makeover for an idea of space saving with modern design. It's simple little well thought out ideas that make a home look special and if you work on your designs on paper, you can come up with some great ideas.

Invest in good lighting fixtures

Strategic lighting is an inexpensive way to instantly change the feel of a room; so if you have money to spend, make sure to invest in good lighting fixtures. You can use a classy floor art to light up a dark area or if you have interesting wall art, use a spotlight to bring attention to that. You can also create an intimate relaxing setting by using low wattage light bulbs in your bedroom or living room.

DIY artwork

You don't need to spend a fortune to decorate those walls with precious artwork. If you want to bring attention to your drab walls, find inspiration and create your very own DIY artwork. A couple of large framed black and white family photographs would look gorgeous on your living room or bedroom wall.

Work with what you have

For someone on a tight budget, the best fixtures and home accessories are those that you already have at home. Before spending money on new fabric or linen, make sure to do an inventory of home items that you can use in your design. You'll never know what kind of interesting home accessories you already have lying around.

Chapter 7: Preparing Your Space for an Uplift

When you assess a room that you want to update, you need to see the actual measurements on paper and also see what it looks like empty. Often, you have so many items in a room that it obscures what you could actually do with that room. If it's at all possible, try to empty the room so that you can have a good look at the shape of the room and decide from there exactly what you want to do with it. It's always easier to work within a room that has been cleared out. Even if this means placing the furniture into the garage for the time being, you get a better shot at designing your room in a more efficient way if it's empty.

Drawing out the dimensions

If you can treat yourself to a booklet with graph paper, drawing out the dimensions of the room gives you a better idea of what you have to play with. For example, you need to mark out where the windows are, where you have fixtures which cannot be moved, where you need any electrical work done, since this would need to be done before the decoration stages. Planning your space helps you to save money long term because you are able to see exactly what you have and buy or refurbish items which will make the room look more modern and updated without flooding the place with items that are too large.

Mark the measurements of the room onto the plan, so that you know how wide the window openings are, where radiators are placed as these cannot be moved and will constrict what furniture you can place in the room. Mark doorways.

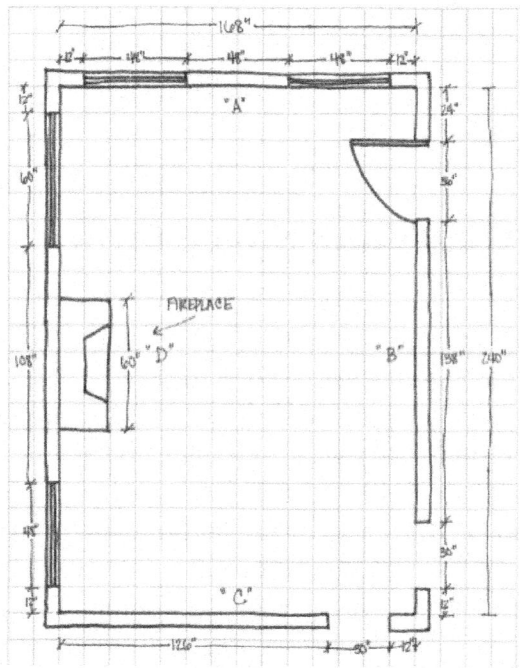

As you can see, the measurements are important and help you to plan out your room. Image from Flicker by Home Designing

Natural light

The natural light within a room is vital to how the room looks. You may have had old fashioned drapes which do not pull back entirely to the rebate edge which means that you may actually be losing natural light. In this day and age, it's a great look to let the light shine into the room. Perhaps you can replace old heavy drapes with linens which allow that light to shine through. Lightweight linen curtains come in all different colors and are reasonably cheap to buy these days, so you may find that you can update the look of the windows and give yourself all the light that you need at the same time. Alternatives could be linen curtains made from lining fabric, which is always going to be cheaper, but which will also let the light get into the room.

Flooring

If you have not updated a room for a long time, you may find that the flooring that you are using is very outdated. Many people who remove old carpet find that underneath that carpet is a wealth of history. Great floor boards which were thought of as unfashionable in the past are in vogue big time. If you find that you have wooden floorboards, it really won't cost you a fortune to do them up so that you have a finished floor. The hire of a sander and a bit of work and you can make the flooring look pretty good. The imperfections that you find are part of that flooring add character, so don't be too worried about them. If you use oriental style rugs on wooden flooring, these look superb.

If, however, you do need to replace the floor covering and are working on a particularly tight budget, there are options. You could make the whole room look lighter and airier by having a light colored flooring and laminate may be worth considering. If you do consider laminate, don't go for the lowest price as this won't be good quality. If you look for prices mid-range, you can get some great bargains and they are so easy to lay yourself. However, for a child's bedroom or guest room, you may want to consider the linoleum which is available today as it is cushioned for comfort, easy to lay and can give you a really nice surface which is easy to keep clean.

Looking at your lighting

If the lighting in the room is not making your space look nice, you can of course change shades, but what about getting recessed lighting? This relatively cheap form of lighting is worth considering because it gives such great light which can be adjusted to suit the moment. Thus with dimmer switching and recessed lights, the room takes on a whole new look.

It's important to look at all alterations which are going to be made to the electrical installations within a room before considering decorating it. While the room is empty is the ideal time to assess this and to have an electrician give you a quotation for this type of work. It may be cheaper than you may imagine and it's always worth talking to the electrician about different possibilities as some alterations will be cheaper than others. He knows where the wiring for that room comes from and will thus have a better idea of what he can do without it costing you too much.

Taking off old wall coverings

This may look like a daunting task but taking off wallpaper is not as hard as you may imagine. With the room empty, you do need to cover the floors to protect them from any dampness and also from slipping on wet wallpaper. For this task, you will need a bucket of warm soapy water, a sponge and a scraper. If your wallpaper is vinyl finished, there is a tool that you can use to grate the surface of the paper so that the water that you sponge onto the paper goes right through all layers. Ask at your hardware store as this is a very inexpensive item and you will use it a lot. After having scraped the surface of the paper, soak an area with soapy water and allow the water to penetrate. If you try removing the paper too soon, you will find it tough going, but if you wait long enough, this will peel off very easily. If one area isn't ready to peel yet, work on another area, adding water so that you work in a rotation.

When peeling off old wallpaper, some of it will come away in large chunks. Have waste disposal bags available and place these easy pieces into the bag straight away. In fact, when you peel paper, get used to binning the paper as you work, so that you do not cause areas to become slippery under where your steps have to stand.

You will find that the paper removes fairly easily, but that there will be little bits left behind. This is normal. When you have finished the whole room, go back over the walls with a clean damp cloth and use your scraper to remove these. They will become yellow when wet and you should be able to see them clearly. The reason it's so important to remove all of the little bits is that they will show through whatever new wall covering you choose to use in the room.

Sugar soaping the paintwork

This is all part of the preparation process and doesn't take long. The paintwork including the architrave around a door, the base boards and the windows will all need to be washed down so that the years of dirt of dust is removed ready for rubbing down the surface for paint. Sugar soap is semi abrasive and helps to give you a really clean start, so that when you work on the paintwork, it will look as if performed by a professional. That saves you money and gets you good results.

The room is now prepared and you need to decide upon the style that you want to create in that room. In the following chapter, there are some details which may help you to decide upon an interior decorating style that is suited to your room. Look through the ideas and also look up images on Pinterest or in magazines that give you an idea of what you can do with that room. You'd be surprised at the results you can get without having to pay professionals to do the work for you.

Chapter 8: Knowing More about Different Interior Design Styles

If you're starting an interior design project, one of the first questions that you need to ask yourself is, "what style should I choose?" It doesn't matter if you're decorating a condominium unit, or a 3 bedroomed house, picking out a specific style can make decorating a lot easier.

If you want to be able to put together a well-designed room, you need to consider 3 things before picking out a specific style. First, it should look well with the rest of the house, second, it should be appropriate for the space, and third, it should reflect your personality and taste. Don't be afraid to mix and match different styles if you're going for a unique and vibrant feel. To get started, here are just a few interior design styles that you can draw inspiration from.

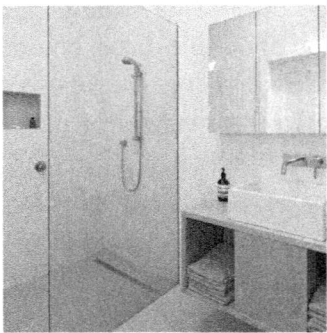

Look how the modern lines are used in this bathroom. The bathroom is still very functional but not fussy or busy. That means that decorative elements are kept to a minimum and that the overall look is a clean one. Towels can be blended in with the color of tiling if that's something you want to incorporate and the style of faucets used is simple and unfussy. Image from Flicker by Styulish Susan

Contemporary

The contemporary aesthetic gives off a trendy welcoming feel, making it perfect for people who like to be in style. Colors and furnishings are basic and bare, but bold at the same time. Open space is an important element to this style, so clutter and extra details are absolute no-nos. Geometric patterns and unique furniture pieces are used to add interest to this style.

This kind of styling is popular today for living spaces because it affords individuality and it doesn't cost the earth to create a space that is contemporary in style.

For example, you can have individual artwork items that give it boldness and these don't have to be expensive. It's where you place things and the colors that you choose that help to pull this style off.

You could hunt out contemporary items in an antique or second hand store and you may even possess contemporary seating but have not really been able to see it because the room was too busy with other things. Look how the single chair in this picture stands out because the background is minimalistic and the contrasting colors used are plain. Image from Flicker by Home Stylish

Urban

Urban interiors are perfect for those who want to combine living and working spaces together. This is a style that is often seen in converted buildings like renovated warehouses or studio apartments. Making use of open wide spaces, the urban style showcases creative use for exposed structural materials. You'll also see a lot of industrial materials like steel pipes and refurbished pallets used as furnishings. Creativity is key if you want to pull off that urban feel for your multifunctional space.

This kind of style is usually divided into separate living areas, not by walls but by clever placement of furnishings and by the decorative elements that are used so that those different areas can be distinguished, one from another. For example, a dining space within an urban interior may be colored in a different way and have different lighting to the general living space. This adds focal interest to an area within a large space and makes it feel more intimate.

Classical

Classical design is based on symmetry and balance and is heavily influenced by classic Greek and Roman design. One thing that really defines the classical style is the use of a focal point in the room such as a fireplace or a large piece of furniture like a piano. Furniture and decor are then arranged around the focal point to highlight it. Natural colors and textures are preferred in this style to give it a warm feel. Fabrics used are more traditional, adding to the room's overall elegance.

Classical styling may also be that style of decoration which is in character with the era in which the building was constructed. Many people like to bring a home back to how it would have been originally presented, as fashions have changed over the years. Stripping back the layers of superficial decoration can often give very pleasing results because many of the classic features have been hidden because of changes in fashion. However, truly classic style will never really go out of vogue.

The tradition of fireplaces and shelving actually can look very smart indeed and you may have alcoves that you can use to add all that extra storage space without having to buy expensive furniture but

instead, using built in items. Images from Flicker Style and Elegance

Art Deco

Art deco is generally sleek, with touches of drama in furniture and decor pieces. The feel is very glamorous with lots of industrial metals and lacquered wood accents. To add to its dramatic feel, black or a darker shade of purple is used as the main color. In order to counteract the dark feel of the color palette, table lamps with frosted shades can be used. This design is known for being intentionally overly decorated with bold colorful wall art, bronze accessories, and etched glass vases.

If you like Art deco, then think angles because it's usually the angles that give away this styling. Think dramatic. Think theatrical.

You may even be able to find pieces that are suitable to this style in second hand stores and they may just be the pieces that make the difference between bland styling and definitive Art deco. Image from Flicker by Art Deco Home

Retro

When old trends make a comeback, it's often with a modern twist. This style may be difficult to recognize at first look, but if you see classic pieces and colors that remind you of a specific era, then you'll know it's retro. Whether you're going for 50s Americana or 70s disco, make sure to use materials and artwork that are reminiscent of the time. To keep the look modern and up to date, try not to saturate the space with too many nostalgia pieces.

The retro look brings back old type styling in cookers or refrigerators and colors that are pastel blended with other colors such as used in the tiling in this image. Image from Flicker by Finish Furniture

This kind of style can be something from your past or from TV shows that are in the retro style. If you think of the television series of the Fonz, this is the type of dateline that you are aiming for with furniture in the style used at that time and light fittings which are retro as well.

Country

If there were two words to describe the country style, those two words would be cozy and homey. Think cottage living in the countryside. Rich in nature inspired and floral patterns, this style gives off that warm, comfortable feel, with the tendency to become cluttered with all the bulky wood furniture. But even though it may look and feel dated, the textured walls and the unfinished wooden pieces give this style that rustic feel.

Country styling is quite easy to reproduce without having to spend too much. For example, the colors that you choose for your painting can make all of the difference to the way the room is presented. A rustic country style would typically use colors that are warm, earth tones so that the overall impression that people get when they look at the interior of the house is warmth and comfort.

Minimalist

The minimalist style originated from the concept of Zen philosophy. It simplifies living spaces so that you end up with an open organized area. The sense of order adds to the visual interest of this style. Cool colors are used with white to give it that clean feel. The minimalist style is often used in large spaces and uses only a few essential furniture pieces. Natural light in this setting is used as a feature and is highlighted in the choice of minimal decor.

One of the features of this style of interior is that there isn't any clutter. Things have their place and everything is put away so that the overall look is uniform and neat. Minimalistic styling is easy to keep clean because the style positively encourages tidiness. If you like this style, it's unlikely that you would be someone who likes clutter anyway. Essential to this style is good storage so that you can have as many possessions, but don't need to be constantly surrounded by them.

Victorian

If there was a style that was the complete opposite of minimalism, it would be Victorian. This style is flamboyant, luxurious and excessive with the decorations. But even though it might feel like there's a lot going on, it doesn't look cluttered. The Victorian style color palette mixes deep hues with pastels and neutrals, serving as the perfect backdrop for the heavy wood furniture. Walls and floors are kept bare as much as possible in order to contrast the decorative features of the style.

The Victorian era was one when decoration was beginning to flourish in the interior of a home. Pictures were extravagant in presentation. There was also an elegance about the furnishings which were used and you can recreate this style using second hand furniture which can be used to dictate the color scheme used. Window seats were a popular theme in Victorian houses since many had bay windows and cushions were certainly popular.

Georgian

The Georgian style is characterized by elaborately carved furniture and luxurious fabrics. The color palette of this style may be particularly pale, but the rich mahogany furniture makes up for it. Patterns and colors of the drapes are subtle with hints of Chinese designs in the prints. You'll also find Chinese porcelain lamps and cabriole legs as pleasant decorative surprises. The fireplace is often the heart of the room so more often than not, furniture is arranged to achieve radial balance.

In the Georgian era, people were a little more extravagant with their interiors, but these days you can reproduce that look relatively cheaply. Cornices, for example, were in vogue and so were chair rails. These can be installed these days relatively cheaply since the cornices are made of polystyrene rather than plaster, and a homeowner can easily install them without a great deal of expertise. Chair rails were useful not only for the function of protecting the wall from the chairs being rubbed against them, but also as a decorative element since you can decorate above and below chair rail level with different colors to get even more visual interest or to make a tall room look more in proportion.

Rococo

This interior design aesthetic features a lot of intricate and ornate details found in its decor and furniture pieces. Rococo is rich and flamboyant and isn't apologetic about it. You'll also see a lot of gold painted furnishings contrast with the subtle pastel walls. Curves and spirals are dominant design elements, giving rococo style a hint of playfulness. You'll find multiple large mirrors on the walls, as well as expensive ornately framed paintings of people or landscapes.

Rococo is easy to imitate because there are so many variations of this style and you can pick up a lot of items that fit into the style of your room from reclamation yards or from second hand stores.

By now, you probably already have a good idea on how you can decorate your home in the style you want. But before you get started, don't forget to read up on the last chapter on interior design tips, especially written for beginners as well as familiarizing yourself with techniques which are shown in the chapters that lie ahead.

Creating a style means getting the room ready for that style and then creating a design clipboard, collecting all the ideas that you can, ready to use to create the style you have chosen.

Chapter 9: Gathering your Samples and Making a Design Clipboard

Now that you have an idea of the style that you are looking for, do browse through magazines for ideas and clip out any pictures that you think will help you in your search for the perfect style.

You need a clipboard with your plan attached to it and the things that you need to start seeking are ideas that you want to put into practice within that space. You will first need to decide upon the color palette that you will use for the room as this is vital to your choice of fabrics and accessories and paint colors, as well as ornament and wallpaper.

If you have items which are upholstered, then you will need to take digital photos of these if you know that the upholstery is not something that you are going to change. Often you have to work with what you have and use the main colors of items which will not change to balance with any new colors that you introduce to the room.

For example, you may have a dark blue armchair, but that doesn't mean your whole room has to be blue. You have to choose clever color schemes which blend with the blue rather than make the whole area blue. Look at the image below and you will see what is meant by this. In fact, very little about the room in question is blue.

The designer of this room has cleverly incorporated neutral colors and then used the blue chairs as a highlight which is balanced out wonderfully with the picture windows. Yes, there are little touches of blue in the decoration, such as on the table, though the overall color scheme is not blue per se. Thus, you can pick colors which blend nicely with the upholstered items that you have and take samples of colored fabric and paints to try and bring the whole look together. Image from Flicker by Stylish Home

The paint colors will be important, but it's the overall look that matters. As you add a fabric or a color stand back and look at the overall balance of the look and decide whether your choices are good choices or nor. You can mix patterns, but be careful how you do this as if you have too much pattern, this can distract the eye from the overall design. A design board is basically a collection of ideas that you want to put together. You can add to it or take away from it but at the end of the day, what you are looking for is perfect balance to suit the style that you are trying to create and it doesn't always take spending a lot of money to create a wonderful style.

In the above image, the designer has put together different fabrics and color swatches together with ideas from magazines and this is the kind of thing that you are trying to create. See the groups of fabrics. The designer is grouping items, which means that not all of them need be used, but by moving around the swatches, it gives the designer a better idea of what would work well together and what won't. That's important. The fabrics may be used for cushions or something like that and the basic colors of your room may be fairly bland. These cushions can add zest to the room and a lot of great interest when someone looks at a room. The big plus with adding cushions is that the amount of fabric that you need to create them is a relatively small amount so that this kind of décor does not have to cost a great deal. Image from Flicker by Julenne

Chapter 10: 50 Interior Design Tips for Beginners

Whether you're decorating just one room, or your entire home, creating the perfect space can be a fulfilling experience. It shouldn't just be pleasing to the eye, your space should represent who you are, and at the same time serve its purpose in your home. If you've always wanted a home that you can be proud of, start with these foolproof interior design tips, especially put together for beginners.

Tip 1 – Color schemes

Pick out happy colors for rooms that you regularly use for entertaining. Bright colors are awesome for stimulating conversation. They are also colors which will catch the light and make the room look warm. Happy colors are all the natural colors and if you are a little frightened of being too bold, stick to using bolder colors in smaller areas, using more subtle shades in areas which are larger. You can always add artwork to walls which are bland and use the feature color for the picture frames, thus bringing harmony to the whole look.

Tip 2 – Pieces that fit your space

Before investing in a chandelier, make sure that it works with the room not just style-wise, but proportion-wise as well. You don't want the piece overwhelming the room. This isn't just with chandeliers. This also means when you buy any item to fit a room. For example, if you have a small guest room and fit a large double bed, it will automatically shrink the space. Try a three quarter size bed and it instantly makes the room look bigger.

Size is important because it means proportion. If you have a small wall and hang a huge picture, it's okay as a focal point, but if you were to do that on all the walls, it would look out of proportion to the room. Thus, before investing in anything which is size detailed, think out your space and know that the size is correct for the space in which the item will be placed.

Tip 3 – Buy chairs and table separately

Looking for a new dining set? Find chairs that will look great with the table. Pay attention to scale and make sure that the seat height is compatible with the table height. You may be able to find bargains in an antique or second hand furniture store, but do be sure to try the table and chairs together before parting with your money. Similarly, furniture stores may have items that can be bought separately which you like. Place the items together before making the purchase and do try the chairs for comfort with the table.

Tip 4 – Careful choice of lighting

Lighting can make or break your space. If you want to get it just right, check how your rooms look with natural light and try to replicate that. If you want to create two separate spaces within a room, that can be achieved by having focused lighting in the dining area of the room which hangs just above the table and thus draws attention to that area. This is great for when you have guests and need not cost a fortune. The lighting in a child's bedroom should be practical. Perhaps the child will not be too keen on the darkness. Thus, use a bedside lamp which is themed for a child and as the child grows, you can simply update the lamp.

Bathroom lighting should be relaxing. This is an important room for seeing yourself as well. If you can use subdued lighting for the bathing area, you could also have spotlighting for near the mirror so that you have adequate light for makeup or for shaving.

Tip 5 – Use of illumination

Light your favorite things in a room rather than just the space. Don't just use lighting to brighten up a room; use it to show off your personality. For example, if you have artwork or ornament that cries out for lighting, then this doesn't have to be expensive, but can look very chic indeed. If you have a favorite set of glassware, having this on shelves which are illuminated lets the light reflect from the glass and can look very attractive indeed.

The lighting used on this picture is first rate, because what it does is help to show off the artwork and the home designer has added pottery to go with the color of the painting so that the overall look is very warm indeed. This small additional lamp isn't expensive but it's certainly worth thinking about if you want to show off items as a feature in a room. Image from Flicker by Lightning and Fixtures

Tip 6 – Use muted colors

Muted walls, floors, and sofas act as the perfect canvas for any room design. Invest in classic pieces and colors and indulge in trendy items like pillows and lampshades as these will add great interest value. Rugs are also an addition which adds richness. Sometimes, you can get away with bland coloring on the overall design if you bring in accessories which show off the room to perfection.

Tip 7 – Using pieces with historic interest

If you want to add interest to a room, incorporate one item from a different era and showcase it as the room's show piece. This could be a rocking chair in front of a fireplace. It could be a blanket box at the end of a bed or a four poster bed. Having something of historic value really does add to the way that the room is seen by people and you may just want to use items passed down through the family. An alternative is to find items at garage sales and spruce them up and use them as center pieces, because there certainly are bargains to be had.

If you don't have heirloom pieces, then why not paint a piece of furniture as a center piece. Sometimes, that newly painted item can really set the room off and look very interesting indeed. You can even try your hand at different finishes since there is so much special effect paint on offer these days that's it's easy to create a masterpiece for the fraction of the price that one would cost you, had you bought it already finished to your requirements.

Tip 8 – Golds, silvers and metallic colors

When utilized tastefully, metallic shades like gold and silver can add a luxurious feel to any room. These can be used sparingly in a dining room to blend with the colors of the edges of your porcelain, or used in a child's room to give an ultra-modern feel. Perhaps the best place for metallic is in a computer room where you want to create a space age environment and this can look very good as well as helping keep dust at bay. A desk with a metallic worktop or a wall behind the computer in metal can look fantastic.

Even the incorporation of metal in a kitchen helps to give the kitchen clean lines. Some of the world's most famous kitchens incorporate stainless steel worktops and these can look stunning. If you cannot afford them, then you can add utensils to the kitchen on racks so that they are seen as part of the overall picture.

Tip 9 – The rule of threes

Always decorate in threes. Hanging family photos on the wall? Hang three! Placing throw pillows on your couch? Do it in threes. Decorative elements in threes just look more polished. This could equally apply to candles on the dining table or the mantle. This is a great look and even three vases with separate flowers in them placed on a dresser can look more stunning than a single vase.

Tip 10 – The addition of rugs

A statement rug in your chosen color palette can really help put together the look of a room. It doesn't just add a splash of color, it can also be functional and give the room a warmer look. When choosing rugs, if you can't afford the authentic, look on websites such as eBay because you may be able to afford more rug than you thought possible. Rugs add a huge value to a room and also give the room a feeling of comfort.

Tip 11 – Use mirrors wisely

Mirrors should be a staple in your room design. Mix and match different shapes and sizes to create a dramatic focal wall. The other reason that mirrors are so important to design is that they instantly create more light in a room especially if they are placed to reflect window light. They thus make the space look larger than it is and that's a great tip for those who have small homes and want the big home feel.

Tip 12 – Family photos

Pick out your most favorite photographs and have them framed. Turn a blank and boring wall into your very own memory gallery. This is a great area to have in any room but the family room and the hallway come to mind. Hallways are usually fairly bland and a gallery of family photographs up the stairway can look stunningly beautiful, if you choose the right frames and make the look very intentional rather than merely an accidental gathering of images.

Colors and styles of frames will help to draw the gallery look together. Image from Flicker by Picture and Frames

Tip 13 – Buy quality

Designer branded furniture pieces aren't always well made or comfortable. If you're going to invest in expensive furniture, make sure to choose a piece that will last you a lifetime. You can often find wonderful furniture in second hand or antique markets but don't part with your money too easily. You may just get it at a price which you decide upon rather than paying the price on the ticket. Auctions are another good place to find furniture which other people don't want any more but be sure to examine the piece thoroughly before you place your bids.

Tip 14 – Invest in artwork

A few key pieces of artwork can really spruce up your home so invest in a few that you really love. Move them around from time to time to give rooms a whole new look. Artwork is value because it means that your home looks more polished and finished. If you cannot afford originals, then prints are just as good, but you do need to have these framed nicely so that they don't look cheap. The presentation of pictures is everything. Give them a head start by choosing frames which really do complement the style that you are trying to create.

Tip 15 – Add period drama

If you have architectural details built in your home like dramatic stairways and hallways, highlight these features with well-planned lighting. These are parts of the past but they are probably what endeared you to the place when you bought it. Highlight them and let that historical look come out. Fireplaces which have been hidden behind drywall for years may be stunningly beautiful and can be featured as a focal point in a room. Old cornicing painted looks wonderful and can give character to a room.

Tip 16 – Plump up the cushions

You can never have too many cushions in your home. Purchase them in bulk to get a good deal and use your design board to look at all the fabrics together. If you can't get samples, photograph the fabric and look at them from a short distance to see which colors work best together. In a shop situation, lay the chosen cushions out together and see what the overall effect is. Cushions are a cheap investment. They add color and style to a room without having to spend a great deal of money, but without them, a room can look bland and uninteresting.

Tip 17 – De-clutter

Whenever you feel like your space is starting to get cluttered, take a moment to purge items that just don't belong in the overall look of the room. You simply can't showcase a room well if there's clutter everywhere. That is one of the reasons that we suggest you empty a room before you decorate or remodel it. This gives you the bare bones of the room and you can introduce pieces one at a time after the decoration is done, deciding which pieces would be better elsewhere. If it doesn't add to the style of the room, it doesn't belong there.

Tip 18 – Keep window treatments simple

Keep window treatment for big beautiful windows simple and elegant. Always make sure that you have enough sunlight coming in during daytime. To see how much light you could be getting pull the drapes away from the window recess and watch how the light transforms a room. Heavy, overstated drapes can kill a good design and make it look old fashioned. It's much more fashionable to use linens that allow the light to pass through into the room.

Tip 19 – Color tips

When deciding on your color palette, always make sure to add a couple of neutrals into it. No matter how bold your chosen colors are, your color palette is guaranteed to stay elegant if there's at least one neutral. This may look boring on its own but what happens is that you use feature colors on small walls, for example, and use the neutrals for ceiling and the other walls. Then bring the look together with artwork, photographs or decoration which actually brings the featured color onto the neutral wall tastefully.

Look at how neutral the color scheme is in the above picture. The designer has used the yellow painted furniture and picked up the color in the flowers in the room. Bright colors have been introduced, but the basic backdrop of the design is a neutral color which really gives the whole space light. Image from Flicker by Interior Style

Tip 20 – Make your home a treasure trove

Display only what you love. Anything less would just be a waste of space. If that means finding new homes for things which are perhaps functional rather than decorative, then that's the best way to deal with items that don't do the room justice.

Tip 21 – Move things around

To see a room's full potential, don't be afraid to rearrange furniture every once in a while. This will help you see things from a different perspective. Therefore, it's not a good idea to have too much fixed furniture which doesn't allow you this pleasure.

Tip 22 – Update furniture

Have an old piece of furniture that you can't part with? Update it with new fabric. It's a quick fix that will instantly update its look. Before you do this, make sure that the furniture is not valuable as this may actually lose you money, but if it's simply shabby and needs to be chic, then upholstery is the way to go. This can be done easily to dining chairs, armchairs and even sofas. When you take off the old upholstery, use the pieces that are removed carefully as your pattern for new fabric, but don't buy fabric which is not intended for upholstery as it won't last long.

Tip 23 – Use shapes that enhance your space

For smaller rooms, choose round tables so that space flows better. Minimize hard edges if you want a room to look more spacious.

Tip 24 – Simple and functional

If you have a limited budget for furniture, make sure that you invest in simple and functional pieces. Resist the urge to splurge on embellished furniture as these can be hard to mix and match. Simplicity of furniture style means that you get to decide what the overall look is all about rather than letting fussy furniture dictate to you what it should go with.

Tip 25 – Change the handles

Change up furniture hardware with some statement pieces. The extra bling can glam up boring furniture. Knobs and knockers are relatively cheap and you can get some great looks from a small investment, using your existing furniture but giving it new fixtures and fittings.

Tip 26 – Colors for a warmer room

When choosing colors for rooms with natural light, go for jewel tones. This will really brighten up the space. It also makes the room look warmer. White may be the preference, but white in a large space with good light can actually look cold.

Tip 27 – Buy sufficient materials

Always make sure that you have all your materials before starting a job. Create a list of your needs for the preparation of the room, for the painting and for the additional touches. Stay within your budget. If buying wallpaper, make sure that all rolls have the same dye lot because if they do not, you will see a slight variation in color. It's better to order one roll too many than not enough.

Tip 28 – Use your design clipboard

It helps to have a color scheme ready before you get started on decorating a room. It helps you stay focused on the look that you want to achieve. That's why we insisted that you create a design clipboard. This way the look that you end up with is not accidental, but completely planned to look great. It's worth taking the extra time to do this as the end result will look more professional.

Tip 29 – Look for natural inspiration

Draw inspiration from nature and art instead of trends. You'll never go wrong with nature inspired tones and designs. Look for inspiration in magazines and you will see that natural art really does look comfortable when in place, rather than trendy art which may look dated within a short space of time. Nature is never out of fashion.

Tip 30 – If in doubt, leave it out

If you have doubts about a certain pattern, just move on. You have to either love it or hate it, and there is no in-between. The point is that you will be looking at those designs every day and if you don't have enthusiasm for them on the first day, imagine what it will feel like when you have to see those designs daily. Don't compromise. Neutral paint and a picture looks better than walls done in a color or style that you are not sure about.

Tip 31 – Add textures

Add depth and interest to a room by using different textures. A room that looks too polished can come off as boring and unwelcoming. For example, you can introduce textured cushions, rugs or even wall hangings at a relatively small cost and these add real wealth to a room's design.

Tip 32 – Ceiling colors

Try painting your ceiling in a light shade of your room's color. This will help make the room taller and airy. If you have sloping ceilings, you can paint these the same color as the wall to give the room unity.

Tip 33 – Using neutrals

If you're still unsure of the colors you want to use in a room, always start off with neutral walls. Starting off with a blank slate allows you to add whatever pattern and color you want later on. If you are a little afraid of a color, you can always make your base coat lighter than intended and build this up on the final coat.

Tip 34 – Paint bold pieces

You can up cycle an old table or chair by painting it in a bold color. This can be the perfect project for you if you're looking to change up your furniture without spending much. If you are nervous about being that bold, choose an item for the room and paint that. This could be a chair for a child's bedroom or a dresser for a guest bedroom. Give yourself time to get confident with painting. Remember that you can always repaint it if you are unhappy with the results.

Tip 35 – Using color to calm

Desperate for a good night's sleep? Use pale shades of color for your bedroom. This way, you won't feel stimulated before bedtime. Lighting is also important. If you can have dimmer switches, these don't cost a lot and you can turn the light down to relax your eyes, with bedside lamps for reading so that you have the choice.

Tip 36 – Layering the look

Keep your color palette simple and just add drama by layering your room with different materials, textures, and lighting. Try not to play it too safe, when it comes to picking out decor for your room but if you need to gain more confidence, that color can be added to your design board first, so that you can get a good idea of how the different colors will go together when the room is painted.

Tip 37 – Add vibrance

Have a lot of vibrant pieces and patterns that you want to incorporate in your design? Then keep walls and window treatment subtle. This will help keep the room looking classy, with that element of fun. Remember the importance of focal points as these vibrant pieces really can make a style statement.

Tip 38 – Try prints

Don't be afraid to play around with prints. To maintain the room's look, choose different prints in different shades of the same color. This can be for your upholstery, cushions, drapes and wall hangings. Printed fabrics can be very attractive.

Tip 39 – Opposing textures

Opposing texture can create a stylish contrast for your space. Utilize it well. Look at this mixture of cushions and you will see what is meant by that. You don't have to be boring in your style. Add colors and patterns with panache.

It is the overall color that will always shine through, but look how colors were used in this design. They cleverly verge upon a rust color and give an overall impression of harmony. Image from Flicker by Home and Style

Tip 40 – Use of grey

Grey may not look like an exciting color, but adding it to your bold color palette can generate a very interesting look for your room. It's the best color to build your color palette on if you like softer colors. White is very stark and grey gives you a little more softness which can be added to with colors such as blue, yellow, pink and even green. If you are mixing your own paints, keep a stock of black coloring because it flattens a color and makes it very suitable to add with grey.

Tip 41 – Design and color for class

If you want to create a comfortable and livable space, combine a subdued color palette with a symmetrical room arrangement. It's the easiest way to create harmony in your design.

Tip 42 – Use artwork for inspiration

Find inspiration in your favorite artwork. You can easily build a look for the room by taking note of color shades and details that are used in the artwork. If this is a favorite piece and you use that as a guideline, you won't go too far wrong in creating a look around that artwork, rather than fitting the artwork into a particular style.

Tip 43 – Calm the ceilings

Use matt paints on ceilings as these are non-reflective and can create a calm environment much more easily than using high gloss finishes. In fact, high gloss can make a room look big and impersonal as well as showing up all the flaws in your walls or ceilings.

Tip 44 – Use of florals

Floral elements can liven up a space instantly. Make sure you have at least one floral piece in a room. If you can't bring yourself to use floral wallpaper, then simply having an artwork vase with flowers can add warmth to the design.

Tip 45 – Mix new with old

Don't be afraid to mix old with the new, bold with the simple when it comes to buying pieces for your room. Often this works well as modern and old go well together to create an overall individual style.

Tip 46 – Creating interest

Line the back of your bookcases with your favorite printed wallpaper. It doesn't just add color to the space, it also adds depth. If you are not keen on this idea, arrange your bookcases so that they are filled to brimming with books of similar sizes and the color of the books is arranged so that it looks wonderful and adds a rich layer to the room.

Tip 47 – Dark colors

If you're going to use dark colored paint, make sure that it has a sheen finish. Flat dark paint will only make your room look depressing and boring. The best finish for this kind of paint is eggshell which is subtle and satin rather than shiny and too bold. When using this in dark colors, make sure that you walls are prepared correctly before painting.

Tip 48 – Natural light

When choosing colors, make sure that you check how they look under 2 kinds of light. Natural and artificial. If you use your clipboard, you can examine this easily in daylight and if you are taking photos of existing furniture, try to take these in good light so that the colors are as accurate as possible.

Tip 49 – Accent colors

Repeating accent colors in your pillows, linens, or floor rugs in different rooms can help connect the whole house together. Don't overdo it, but it can give the home great harmony.

Tip 50 – avoid op-art

Following a black and white scheme may seem easy enough to pull off, but it can get boring really fast. Add texture to prevent the look from coming off as flat. Break the monotonous feel with the use of flower arrangements, layered fabric and natural wood furniture.

Chapter 11: Simple Preparation Tips to Help You to Create Perfect Walls and Ceilings

Although people underestimate the importance of the preparation, it's more important or at least equally important as the finish because you will see if walls and ceilings have not been prepared correctly. Since you are working on a budget, chances are that you are undertaking the work yourself and this may be the first time that you have tackled it. The information below should help you to see how to prepare walls and ceilings so that you get great looks.

Tools required for preparation:

Paint Scrapers in various sizes

Interior filler or spackle

Medium and fine grain sandpaper

Drop cloths

Stepladder

Dust brush

Before you begin to prepare your walls and ceilings, you need to protect the floor beneath where you are working. This is vital because you will create a lot of dust.

Place the drop cloth onto the floor and don't be tempted to use polythene as this is too slippery and your ladder may slip. Cloths which are of decoration quality are the best, but if you don't have these, use old sheets.

Examination of the surfaces

You will need to examine the surfaces of your walls and ceilings to find all of the cracks. These are quite normal in any home. Likely places that they will occur are at the junction between the wall and the ceiling, between the wall and the baseboard and corners of a room. In all cases, you need to scrape out the crack to remove loose debris. Even if the crack looks small, rake it out using the side of the scraper to create a "V" ready to take the new filler.

If you see cracks like this, don't be too worried. Part of the crack is hollow and needs to come down. If you tap it, this will begin to remove it. Bear in mind when you are dealing with cracks such as this, you will need to clean out the surface and brush it before applying plaster and will need to build up a layer of filler at a time, rather than trying to use too much in one hit. Let a small layer dry and then add another as this is much more likely to give you great results.

In the case of hairline cracks, scrape out the crack, sweep it with the dust brush to get rid of loose debris and then fill, using your paint scraper flat against the surface so that the filler goes into the crack but you don't leave excessive amounts of filler as you pull the paint scraper or spackle knife over the surface.

Allow this to dry. This is very important. Before you are able to apply paint to the surface, you need to rub this down with medium and then fine sandpaper so that the surface is completely flat. If you do notice that it needs more filler, then it's more prudent to add this than to ignore the problem hoping that the paint will cover it. It won't.

After the filling has been done and you have sanded down all the areas which have been filled, use a sweeping brush to brush down the walls so that all the dirt is removed from them before paint is applied.

Where baseboard and wall meet

This is always a difficult area, since the baseboard may come away from the wall at any time and it always looks unsightly when there is a gap between the baseboard and the wall. If you are sure that the baseboard is sufficiently fixed to the wall, then you need to use your paint scraper or spackle knife to apply filler between the baseboard and the wall. If you use a dampened cloth what you can do after you have filled the entire strip is run your finger along the top of the filling protected by the cloth, to take off any excess filler and to give you a perfectly smooth finish ready for rubbing down and painting, once it is dry.

The preparation of your surfaces cannot be over emphasized in importance. This gives you a chance to look at the structure of your home and to notice if there are reasons why areas are cracking or whether there are stains appearing on the surface of a ceiling. The reasons may be simple to rectify and may even have been rectified in the past. For example, a leaky seal around a shower or bathtub in the room above may just have meant that water was leaking onto the ceiling.

To get rid of stains on ceilings

The most effective way to hide these unsightly stains is to use an oil based undercoat just on the area which is stained, before you paint the ceiling. This must be given sufficient time to dry.

If you find that the stain still needs more coverage, try a little more undercoat but be patient as this process will be worth your while at the end of the day, because it means your new surface will not be ruined by having the stain seep through your new paint.

Chapter 12: Making Great Savings on Design Elements

The idea of this book is to give you a lot of detail so that you can use this to help in your experience, though this chapter helps you to create you individual style but save money at the same time. We have gone through all the rooms of the house and given you tips as where savings can potentially be made. Remember that all electrical work and plumbing work should always be done by a qualified person who can ensure that the work is done to code. It's important that this is respected so don't try to make savings in these areas as it may be a false economy. The money that you save elsewhere in your design elements will free up more money to help you to use the professionals when appropriate.

Entrance way

This is the first area that people see when they enter your home. Make it bright and airy and a great transition to the rooms that go beyond it. In this area, you can save money by buying paints during sales and making sure that you buy white as your predominant color. Then, add color tubes so that you can mix your own colors. That means that you can create a great color for the entry way and then carry on in the same scheme of color but changing the shade a little for each of the rooms that transitions from the hall.

Family room

This is a room where good planning will help you to make savings. For example, MDF built in cupboards to house all of your entertainment items will be cheap to make and you can paint it to match in with the walls so that it doesn't look out of place. MDF is easy to work with and you can get some great plans for making units or simply work on your own design, buying sufficient MDF to make all the units you need for DVDs, CDs and the actual TV and accessories, so that they are neatly put away and don't depend upon independent furniture items. In fact, built in, they blend into your design in a much better way.

The artwork in the family room can be something you can make. If you like a particular wallpaper but don't want the cost of a dozen rolls, use a frieze and create oblong shapes on your walls and paper within the oblong. It's stunning, it's cost effective and means you can have those designs in your room without splashing out too much.

Dining room

For this area, try to find pieces that go well together in antique stores. A great table doesn't have to cost the earth and chairs which are comfortable with it are also something you can pick up relatively cheaply. The dining room can have additions such as candles to give it atmosphere and if you don't want to spend a fortune on lamps, look at standard lamps in antique stores and simply change the shade to give a whole new look to them. These create ambiance in a dining room area and you won't have to pay extra for the electrician to wire in new lighting.

Kitchen

Use cabinet paint on your cabinet doors, after degreasing them and rubbing them down. There are paints which are specifically made for cabinets and they are worth the investment because they are made to take the bumps that kitchen cabinets will be subjected to by normal wear and tear. You can clean up the handles or even buy new ones at a fraction of the cost of new cabinets and if any of your hinges have dropped, buy new ones and affix them at the same time as you decorate and they will look as good as new.

Tiling in the kitchen often gets marks in the grout lines which look unsightly. You can actually buy tile paint which covers the whole area and can be wiped, so this may be an option. Otherwise, what about cleaning the joints with either a steam cleaning nozzle or by using specific products to get them back to looking great again. If all else fails, you can always use an artist's paintbrush and paint the joints with an oil based matt finish so that they look spotless.

The nursery

An old cot or crib can look every bit as good as a new one if you paint it up with baby friendly paints and add a picture to them. To do this, simply source a picture you like and trace it onto the furniture, painting it with baby friendly paints to give the crib a really up to date look. You can make mobiles which hang above the crib and paint walls in light colors that are calming. An old rocking chair painted in pastel shades could be placed in the room for the nursing mom and the whole room will look newly designed and welcoming.

Children's bedrooms

Let the kids help in the artwork. Why not have a wall devoted to them, using lining paper and old picture frames, so that the kids can draw in the picture frames and create their very own look? You can save an awful lot of money on furniture for kid's rooms by painting up second hand furniture, but be careful not to skimp on things like the mattress since there may be hygiene concerns.

Guest bedroom

Here, be inventive. Imagine yourself staying at your house. Make the room welcoming, but look out at garage sales because you might just find the treasure of a quilt which will give you great guidance in your choice of colors. Wall hangings are another thing you may consider as these can give you real design ideas for the room itself, based on the general colors of the items that you have purchased.

Bathroom

Look for tiles which are end of stock but do make sure that you buy sufficient for your bathroom. Buying a few square meters more is better than simply scrimping and buying exact because you will have breakages during the tiling process, but huge savings can be made by choosing end of lines.

Chapter 13: What Is Feng Shui Decorating?

Feng Shui (pronounced as "fungshway") finds its roots in a holistic world view. It observes all things as well as creatures and considers them a part of a natural order: an environment that is in constant motion and change. Each thing within this order represents an energy value or component. So all of us, everything that surrounds you right now, exist in a landscape that swirls with energy. This same energy flows through you and gives you life-- often referred to as "Chi".

How does this apply to decorating? Feng Shui, when applied to design, allows you to create a space for yourself wherein this energy can flow freely, through you and through everything that is enclosed in that space. It enables you to lay out the environment, which is more conducive for it, making sure that you also receive its numerous benefits.

To put this in perspective, think of an office space that's completely cluttered in files, organizers, drawers and other supplies. Now put yourself in this environment. Does it give you a good feeling? Does it make you feel more motivated? It isn't surprising at all if you answered no. In Feng Shui, this kind of environment suffocates the energy, rendering it static and instead of bringing a sense of lightness, it ends up becoming a weight.

Now think of the same office again, but this time, picture it looking more organized. Sunlight streaming through the window, a clear desk and perhaps a couple of indoor greens in the corners. Doesn't that feel much better? It is as if the room itself is breathing whenever you do. That's the sign of good energy flowing freely. It flows from your environment, through you, so you absorb some of the positivity as well.

To further simplify what Feng Shui actually is, here are some important bits of information about it. Let's start with the common misconceptions about the philosophy itself.

–   It is not a quick way to get rich that would guarantee a sudden, mystical change in your fortune by simply moving around pieces of furniture.

–   It is more than just moving around pieces of furniture. There is a real science to how Feng Shui works.

–   It is not based on superstition, not magic nor a New Age fad that would actually disconnect you from reality and have you change your beliefs in order to make it work.

–   It is not a sect or a religion.

–   It is not something that only the rich can afford.

So now that we have some of the common myths debunked and out of the way, here are a few key information to help you better understand what Feng Shui is and how it can affect you.

− The simplest way of describing Feng Shui would be "the interaction between an individual and his or her environment". Now, taking things a step further, Feng Shui can also be defined as a means for you to harness and influence the energies around usin order to accomplish certain improvements in your life. How? By designing your surroundings to be in complete harmony with the natural energy flow in your living or working space.

− It is also typically referred to as "the art of placement". One of the basic ideas that work behind it would be that how and where you place yourself, possessions and furniture within your environment influence your life experience at varying levels. In this sense, it becomes a way of looking at your environment and yourself in a unique way-- and how these two things can help bring in more comfort, positivity, balance and harmony into your life.

− With that said, it is also the study of the relationship between the environment and the quality of an individual's life. First discovered by the Chinese, they have practiced and applied this philosophy to their daily living. From designing the exterior and interior of a home, to choosing the right site for important buildings. All of which are done in an effort to further enhance, not just harmony, but also success.

Chapter 14: Tips For Decorating Your Home On A Budget

Are you interested in trying out Feng Shui for yourself? Well, for beginners, it's always best to start small. If you're on a budget or don't want to invest too much into something you're still quite unsure of, here are a few budget-friendly Feng Shui tips that are sure to add a bit more harmony into your daily living.

−   Bring in some light. Look at your living room or your bedroom right now, is it getting enough sun during the day? Or does it remain dark and closed off regardless of the hour? Time to change things up and bring in more natural light to your living and sleeping areas. If you're not keen on having no curtains, choose a lighter one that filters the sunlight, but doesn't obstruct it. One with an energizing color that matches your home's theme would be best suited for it.

−   Time to get organized. Declutter any areas that seem to be stuffed with all sorts of things. These places collect bad energy and hinder the natural flow of the good one. Begin by bringing organization boxes. These should be quite cheap and would offer you a storage solution that's also aesthetically appealing. When choosing colors, opt for something that blends in with the area you're putting it in so it doesn't attract any attention.

−   Keep, store, throw away and donate. Now, it's time to sort through your possessions and separate them into four categories. Things you want to keep, things you can store for later, items that you can throw away (broken ones that you can no longer fix) and stuff that you are willing to donate. This is, of course, an extension of the previous decluttering that you've done. In doing this, you're sure to feel much lighter.

−   Opt for dimmer lighting in certain areas of your home. Sure, bringing light in is a good thing for energy flow but at night, it can actually make your space look quite harsh. Invest in affordable lamps that would produce softer light, especially in your bedroom. This would give you a glowing feeling of warmth and give the space a much cozier feel. It will help you sleep better too!

−   Time to get green! Bringing indoor plants will certainly liven up a space. Not only will it add color and texture, but it can also produce calming energy. A couple of corner plants in your living room, a few smaller ones by the kitchen window and maybe even one in your room. These are affordable, but great additions to any space.

- Add a water element. This might be a bit more of an investment than the others, but it all depends on what you're planning to use for it. In any case, adding a water element to any space immediately brings in more calming and positive energy. Small water fountains are often used in Feng Shui, but if you can't find one or don't have the spare budget for it, a small metal basin with some decorative pebbles and filled halfway with water should do the trick. Even a glass bowl would work for this. Place it in your living room and simply change the water every couple of days or so.

So there you have it, a few simple and affordable Feng Shui decorating tips that are sure to help you get started with letting energy move through your home.

Chapter 15: Feng Shui Decorating Ideas For Your Living Room

Since you will be spending a lot of your time in the living room, whether by yourself or while you're entertaining guests, it is important that the energy in this space is free-flowing as well as inviting. However, this is also one of the areas in an average home that people tend to pay the least attention to, thinking that a sofa, a few extra chairs and a big television are all that they really need.

To help you spruce up your living room while making sure it follows Feng Shui, here are a few decorating ideas that you might want to consider.

- Move your main furniture pieces into the empowered position. Your bigger chairs and sofas should face the main entrance of your home, but make sure it isn't completely aligned with it. In doing so, you'll find that people will instinctively sit on the piece of furniture placed in this position. It also opens up the area for better interaction. What if you have limited space? This can be resolved by creating a faux. A tall screen, some plants or even a mirror could help with this. What you want to create is a way for people to see everything that is happening in front of them without worrying about what is behind them, hence the block.

- Disguise your television. The sight of it can be quite distracting and you would want that space to be a sanctuary for peace and calm. By covering it up, you're more able to focus on other things within the area. Having a few books handy is certainly beneficial, even a music player would help you unwind. Make sure there are other, more creative things to do, whenever you're in that room. This would certainly help create a balance within and outside of you.

- Incorporate the five elements in your decoration. Adding objects, patterns and colors from the natural world are also great additions to your living room. If you have a monochromatic scheme or plain walls bordering the space, these are very useful for breaking that apart and adding more texture. Get inspired by the five elements, add bits and pieces of each in different areas of the room. Keep in mind that the key here is balance, so don't add something that's too big or bulky.

- Add mirrors. Mirrors are not only useful for making a room appear much bigger; it is also one of the handiest tools when it comes to enhancing Feng Shui in a specific area in your room. Make sure that it is positioned where it reflects either light or a beautiful view that you want to be seen wherever your guests may be in the living room.

- Add live plants. Greens are great for improving the energy flow, as well as balancing the yin and the yang in a space. For aesthetic purposes, its color also relaxes the eyes and brings in a bit of the outside into your indoor space.

- Always choose more neutral colors for your walls and bigger furniture. This would not only keep the space relaxing and calm, but also reflect natural light beautifully. Add your accent color in the details within your space such as the pillows, small decorations, rugs and so on.

Chapter 16: Feng Shui Decorating Ideas For Your Kitchen

The décor and design of your kitchen is also another way of expressing your personal taste, and must work well with the kind of lifestyle that you have. The Feng Shui aspect of decorating it can be considered as a supplement to the whole, making sure that it is a cozy and well-balanced space where you and your family can have a good time as well.

Here are a few tips for designing and decorating your kitchen while following the philosophies of Feng Shui.

- Begin with clearing out the space. Start with the things you no longer need or have no use for. You can sort these into items that you can give away or throw away. The purpose for this is to declutter the area and give the energy more room to flow.

- Proper lighting. It would be great if you can install windows in your kitchen as this would allow natural light, an important element in Feng Shui. Make sure nothing blocks it and that there are no heavy draperies over it. However, if natural light isn't available, just make sure that the kitchen is well-lit but without using harsh lights.

- When plotting out the location for each of your key kitchen equipment, make sure that they are not in conflict with each other. Refrain from having them in a direct line next to each other.

−   Add some plants! Adding plants to different areas in your home enhances the chi and elevates the mood of the space. For your kitchen, windowsill herbs would be the best option. Not only will you be bringing greens into the area, it could also be used for the different dishes that you'll be making. Let's not forget the aroma that many of these herbs give off, which can motivate you to do more in the kitchen.

−   Keep the art to a minimum. Having one too many things hanging on the walls of your kitchen can be very distracting and also obstruct the continuous flow of energy. Consider having only one or two pieces and make sure they portray themes that are suited for the kitchen. Something festive always brings a positive energy to the space.

−   Organize well. Besides the chi, your own energy matters as well when it comes to the area you're working in. One of the most common sources of frustration for many people is being unable to find what they need when they need it. To avoid this and to avoid building up negative energy, organize all of your tools, ingredients and kitchen equipment properly. Label them, have them where you can easily reach and make sure that you also return them in their proper spots once you're done using any of them.

Chapter 17: Feng Shui Decorating Ideas For Your Bedroom Makeover

Because it is considered by many to be the most important room in a home, making sure that your bedroom is following Feng Shui can certainly bring about significant changes. Whether it be in the amount of stress you carry around or attracting more fortune and love, there are a number of simple yet effective changes that you can do. To help you get started, here are a few tips for you to consider:

- Begin with your bed. Have a solid headboard for it that's either made from wood or has been upholstered well. These two varieties are considered the best as they can balance the combination of being a solid backing while supporting Feng Shui energy for you and the bedroom as well. Whenever you sleep, your body goes into energy repair work and having a solid backing aids in this process.

- Get a good mattress. There are countless different varieties available in the market so when choosing one, make sure you don't scrimp on quality. Find the one that would provide you with the best possible sleep as this can also significantly affect your health and your energy level come the morning. Never buy used mattresses for these have already accumulated energy from its previous owners, something that you wouldn't want in your room where you're most vulnerable at night.

- Position your bed as far from the door as possible. The idea here is that you should be able to see the door from your bed, but it shouldn't be directly aligned with it. This also applies to the door of your patio or balcony, the bathroom door as well as your closet door. Too much chi can flow into the bed if you have it placed directly in front of the door.

- Do not place your bed against a window. Aside from the headboard, you should also have a solid wall behind your bed to prevent energy loss. If you have a window, your personal energy can exit through here, thus leaving you feeling weak and lethargic after a while. It is important that you protect your energy even during slumber.

- Make sure your bed is away from any distractions. The TV, your study desk, the computer-- all of these should be outside of your bedroom or if that isn't possible, far from the area where you sleep. You can also drape something over it, as a way of covering these distractions without taking up too much space by adding a closet to keep them in and so on. These can actually hinder the flow of positive energy to your bed so best to keep them away.

Chapter 18: Methods To Organizing Your Home

When it comes to cleaning your home while following Feng Shui, there are a few things you need to consider and prioritize. Not only would doing so make the work much easier to accomplish, it would also leave you with a more peaceful and harmonious space after. So, shall we get straight to it?

Flow. First off, the flow of a space is important. There needs to be a direct path through which the energy can pass. In order to achieve this, here are a few simple tips.

– Stand in the middle of your living room and start looking around. Are you making full use of the space or does it appear smaller because of the furniture in it? If there are pieces that you can remove, do it. Creating a wider space where the eye can easily see everything would be the best layout for this area. Instead of bulky storage, opt for something more compact and low.

– Are there tangled wires from all the electronics? Untangle them and make sure they stay in place by using plastic clasps. You can also opt to use a wiring tube, which would keep everything organized and hidden from view.

Clarity. When getting organized, this is also something that you must keep in mind. Everything should have its own place and you should be able to easily find the things that you need. To do that:

– Always label your storage boxes. If you're keeping them in cupboards or closets, this would save you a lot of time and allow you to get what you need with ease. It would also be more aesthetically pleasing if you keep the boxes similarly colored.

– Keep your work desk neat. Have storage boxes where you can keep all of your supplies and only leave the most basic and oft-used ones on your table. A clear desk breeds creativity.

Relaxation. Of course, this is very important when it comes to Feng Shui. For one, it produces good energy both in the individual and the space they're in. It's not difficult to achieve either as long as you remember a few key points.

– The TV and the computer shouldn't be in clear view. If you have a way of "hiding" them, always do so whenever they're not in use. Make sure any wires connected to it are hidden as well.

– Always fix your bed in the morning. This should make it more inviting come the evening and can actually help you sleep better. Never have more than the basics on your nightstand. Anything that might clutter it should be stowed away.

Chapter 19: Declutter Your Life & Home in 5 Simple Steps

Think decluttering is a tedious business? Not quite. There are simple ways of removing the clutter from your home, which wouldn't take up more than half an hour (or less!) of your time. The trick is to spread the process throughout the week and once you're done, you'll immediately notice a significant change both in the appearance and energy of your home.

Shall we get started?

- Start with your closet. While getting ready for the day, peruse through your racks. In a single glance, you should be able to tell which of your clothes are getting the least mileage. Move those to the side. Repeat the same with your shoes, purses and accessories. It is likely that there's something off about these items; whether it be that they're uncomfortable and simply not your style. So instead of holding onto them, pack everything up and either sell or give them away.

- Now move to the living room and do the same thing with your books, magazines and stacks of other things you don't really need a lot of or use often. Most of the time, people hoard these things because they think there's some use for them in the future while in the present, it's simply eating up space. Pack those away and decide which ones to sell and which ones to give away.

- Decluttering the kitchen can be a bit trickier, but it can be done. Check for expiration dates on the food in your pantry and in the fridge. Often, many of these would simply go to waste because you didn't get to consume them in time. Also, look for broken things. If they're no longer fixable or useful, time to sell or throw them away.

- Remind yourself that you don't need a whole lot of stuff in your house. If there are things that you can do without or have multiples of, it's time to give some away. It might be difficult to part with it, but once you do, it's as if you've lifted a weight off of the space itself.

- Have you been stowing away things in boxes for years and years hoping they'll come into use one day? There won't be a time for that and other people might find better use for it so start donating the boxes. A good deed and a clutter-free house all in one day!

Chapter 20: DIY Home Decorating Ideas

Home décor need not always be expensive or bought straight from the stores, sometimes all you need are a few good ideas and some extra bits of craft material then you're good to go! To help you get started with this, here are a few tips you might want to consider trying out. All are pretty cheap with very minimal amount of things that you need to purchase.

–   Instead of purchasing mass produced arts from the store, why not try and create your own? So you're not very good with a brush and paint, but you don't have to be to get this done. All you need are three (or more, depending on your preference) square wooden frames and some bits of scrap fabric that would fit over the squares. Just stretch it evenly and secure the fabric well onto the frame. Once done, you can add a silk ribbon behind it for easier hanging. These are a simple, but great way of adding a pop of color to any room in your home. Tip: Use different fabric textures and colors to give the "set" a more dynamic feel.

–   Got used graphic tees that you no longer use? Well, don't throw them away. Instead, use it to wrap your pillows. Simply wrap, tuck and pin them onto your square pillows. Not only are you getting to recycle old stuff, you're also able to save the money that you would have used to purchase a pillowcase. Just make sure your graphic remains centered and right at the front. This should also add a more personal and unique twist to the room you're placing these in.

–   Have artificial flowers that are looking faded? What about figurines that aren't as colorful as they used to be? Perhaps you've also changed your preferences into something more minimal and neutral? Well, you can combine all three and come up with truly unique décor. First off, purchase a couple of spray paints in a color that you prefer. White, black or gold would work best for this project since they would blend in well with any surroundings, but still have an impact. Next, you just need to paint these items completely with your chosen color. Keep things monochrome. Let them dry and put them on display. Against more colorful objects, these would surely lend a look of modernity in any space.

- Decoupage! This might just be the easiest way to reinvent any item that lost its appeal, but you still want to keep. It can be used for refurbishing lampshades, old boxes and even small drawers! You can use any kind of paper for it too: old paperbacks, magazine cut-outs and even your favorite pictures.

Chapter 21: Modern Painting Techniques

Besides picking a color, knowing different modern painting techniques can definitely help you add a bit more flare to an otherwise plain well. If you're looking for something that adds texture and personality into the space then this is something you must certainly employ. In this chapter, we'll talk about some of the most popular varieties.

- Color blocking. The name itself should help you picture what it looks like. This basically involves adding a graphic element to the wall itself. Typically, this uses geometric shapes that dress up the wall, but you can also opt to make use of something more complex such as silhouettes. It can be as minimalist or as playful as your imagination makes. This would be more suited for modern spaces and can be used to create a focal point if you want to highlight a certain area of the house or distract from it. It also works as an alternative to your traditional wall art.

- Stencilling. The modern alternative to the wallpaper. This will certainly add a bit more texture and flare to any wall. The best bit is that there are numerous stencil designs that range from the classic wallpaper based designs to more modern and graphic styles that's sure to make your walls pop. They can be used as side, top or bottom accents if you're looking for more subtlety. You can also use them anywhere, from your doors to even the stairs.

- Strie. The French word for stripe. This faux finish painting technique lends a subtle streaked appearance to the walls. Seen from a distance, it actually appears as if the wall has been covered with texture fabric, particularly denim or silk. This is a pretty versatile style and can be used in any room. Its elegance is well-loved by many and when coupled with more neutral colors, it adds a bit more life to the average minimalist space. However, it is also very adjustable so you'll find that it will suit most of your needs regardless of your house's theme or overall design.

- Color wash. If you're looking for something that's eye-catching, but not as graphic as the first two options then this would be your best bet. This technique creates a soft, cloudlike effect on your walls. Because of its relaxing appearance, this style is often seen in bedrooms, powder rooms and bathrooms in which it lends its dreamy atmosphere. Neutral colors are the best suited for this style.

Conclusion

Now that you have read this book you will have all the knowledge you will need in order to start designing your perfect home. You will have the skill to design your perfect home and get your friends gasping at the sign of it.

The perfect space is just within reach. With a bit of creativity and perseverance, you can turn your boring spaces into works of art that reflect your taste and personality.

I hope that this book was able to help you understand the important principles and elements of interior design. Now that you have all that you need to become a good interior designer, put them into use as often as you can so that it will become second nature to you to come up with the best design solutions every time.

Remember that some of the ideas laid out in this book can be mastered in an instant and some need more time to be practiced and mastered. Be patient, you can master the art of interior design in no time.

From the author

Thank you for purchasing this book.

I really enjoyed writing it, and I've already had some great feedback from readers who enjoyed the book. I hope you too enjoyed it.

I appreciate that you chose to buy and read my book over some of the others out there. Thank you for putting your confidence in me to help you. If you enjoyed the book and you have a couple of spare minutes now, it would really help me out if you would like to leave me a review (even if it's short) on Amazon. All these reviews really help me spread the world about my books and encourage me to write more books!

Sincerely Yours,

Richard Foreman

Let me recommend you to read my other popular books:

A Comprehensive Guide in Quitting Drinking: Stop Drinking and Back to Sober Life

Brain Training: The Ultimate Guide to Increase Your Brain Power and Improving Your Memory (Brain exercise, Concentration, Neuroplasticity, Mental Clarity, Brain Plasticity)

CPSIA information can be obtained
at www.ICGtesting.com
Printed in the USA
BVOW04s2124161216
471088BV00022B/595/P

9 781512 263718